The Giant Book of Simple Facts

by
Jake Jacobs

* * * * *

Published by Jake Jacobs

The Giant Book of Simple Facts
Copyright© 2023 by Jake Jacobs

1.

Herons belong to the family Ardeidae, which includes long-legged, wading birds known for their distinctive appearance and hunting behaviors.

2.

There are more than 60 species of herons found worldwide, inhabiting a variety of aquatic habitats such as wetlands, marshes, rivers, lakes, and coastlines.

3.

Herons are known for their elongated legs, necks, and beaks, which are adaptations for catching prey in water.

4.

The heron's scientific name, Ardea, is derived from the Latin word for "heron."

5.

Herons have excellent eyesight, enabling them to detect movement in water from a significant distance.

6.

One of the most recognizable heron species is the Great Blue Heron, known for its tall stature, bluish-gray plumage, and slow, deliberate movements.

7.

Herons are skilled predators, primarily feeding on fish, amphibians, crustaceans, and insects.

8.

They employ various hunting techniques, including standing still and patiently waiting for prey, stalking, and quick lunging.

9.

Herons often use their sharp bills to impale their prey before swallowing it whole.

10.

Some heron species have specialized feeding behaviors, such as "canopy feeding," where they drop bait onto the water's surface to attract fish.

11.

Herons play an important ecological role by helping to control fish populations in their habitats.

12.

Herons are known for their unique courtship rituals, which can involve elaborate displays of plumage, calls, and dances.

13.

Many heron species are migratory, traveling long distances between breeding and wintering grounds.

14.

Herons are highly adaptable and can be found on every continent except Antarctica.

15.

The smallest heron is the Least Bittern, measuring about 11 inches in length, while the largest is the Goliath Heron, reaching up to 5 feet tall.

16.

Herons are colonial nesters, often forming large breeding colonies in trees, reed beds, or on cliffs.

17.

They build platform nests made of sticks and other materials, usually in elevated locations to protect them from predators and flooding.

18.

Both male and female herons contribute to nest building and incubating eggs.

19.

Herons are known for their guttural calls, which can vary in pitch and intensity depending on the species.

20.

Herons have been depicted in art and literature throughout history, symbolizing patience, elegance, and solitude.

21.

The term "heron" can sometimes be used broadly to include related birds like egrets, bitterns, and night herons.

22.

The feathers of some heron species were historically used in fashion, leading to concerns about their populations and protection.

23.

Herons have long lifespans, with some individuals living up to 20-25 years in the wild.

24.

In ancient Egyptian mythology, the heron was associated with creation and rebirth due to its presence around water bodies.

25.

The heron's ability to stand still for long periods inspired meditation practices, symbolizing patience and focus.

26.

In some cultures, herons are considered symbols of good luck and prosperity.

27.

The plumage of herons can vary widely, ranging from snowy white to various shades of gray, brown, and even black.

28.

Some heron species, like the Green Heron, are known for their colorful plumage and distinct markings.

29.

Herons have specialized adaptations in their neck vertebrae that allow them to quickly extend their necks to catch prey.

30.

Some heron species, such as the Black-crowned Night Heron, are known for their nocturnal feeding habits.

31.

The Gray Heron is commonly found in Europe and Asia, and it has been a symbol of divine messengers in folklore.

32.

Herons have been studied for their abilities to innovate and use tools, such as bait to catch fish.

33.

The Squacco Heron gets its name from its harsh, squawking call.

34.

The Nankeen Night Heron is native to Australia and gets its name from the shade of yellow often found in traditional Chinese fabrics.

35.

The heron's long legs help it wade in shallow water while its body remains relatively dry.

36.

The Little Blue Heron starts off as white during its juvenile phase and gradually changes to blue-gray as it matures.

37.

Some heron species, like the Boat-billed Heron, have unique, broad bills adapted for catching crabs and other prey.

38.

Herons have a sophisticated swallowing mechanism that allows them to swallow large prey without choking.

39.

The Great Egret is known for its striking white plumage and was nearly hunted to extinction for its feathers in the late 19th century.

40.

Some heron species, like the Black Heron, engage in a unique foraging behavior called "canopy feeding," where they create a canopy of wings to block out the sun and attract fish.

41.

Herons are territorial during the breeding season and can engage in aggressive behaviors to protect their nesting sites.

42.

During the 19th century, herons were hunted for their feathers, which were used to adorn women's hats and clothing.

43.

Conservation efforts and the Migratory Bird Treaty Act helped protect herons from overhunting and habitat loss.

44.

The Cattle Egret is known for its habit of following large grazing mammals and feeding on insects that are stirred up by their movement.

45.

The heron's ability to stand motionless for extended periods helps it blend into its environment, making it a successful predator.

46.

Some heron species, such as the Purple Heron, have been featured in various mythologies and folktales as symbols of mystery and elegance.

47.

Herons are known for their complex social behaviors within breeding colonies, which can include courtship displays, territory disputes, and communal chick-rearing.

48.

The Great White Heron, found in the southeastern United States, is a color morph of the Great Blue Heron and is the largest heron in North America.

49.

Herons have been subjects of scientific research to understand their feeding behaviors, migratory patterns, and the impact of habitat loss on their populations.

50.

The survival of heron populations is closely linked to the conservation of wetland habitats, as these areas provide crucial feeding and breeding grounds for these iconic birds.

51.

The hippopotamus, known as "hippo" for short, is a large semi-aquatic mammal found in sub-Saharan Africa.

52.

The name "hippopotamus" comes from the Greek words "hippos" (horse) and "potamos" (river), which translates to "river horse."

53.

Hippos are the third-largest land mammals, after elephants and white rhinos.

54.

Despite their appearance, hippos are more closely related to whales and dolphins than to other terrestrial mammals.

55.

Hippos have barrel-shaped bodies with short legs, a large head, and a massive mouth full of sharp teeth.

56.

Their skin is relatively hairless and can secrete a red, oily substance that acts as a natural sunscreen and moisturizer.

57.

Hippos are known for their powerful jaws, which can open up to 180 degrees, revealing their impressive set of sharp teeth.

58.

Even though they are herbivores, hippos are considered one of the most dangerous animals in Africa due to their territorial and aggressive behavior.

59.

Hippos spend a significant amount of time in water to keep their bodies cool and hydrated. They can stay submerged for several minutes before resurfacing to breathe.

60.

They are excellent swimmers and can move gracefully underwater using their webbed feet to push off the bottom.

61.

Hippos are known for their distinctive vocalizations, including grunts, roars, and honks, which they use to communicate with each other.

62.

Despite their size, hippos are surprisingly fast runners and can reach speeds of up to 20 mph (32 km/h) on land.

63.

Their closest relatives are pygmy hippos, which are smaller and found in West Africa's rainforests.

64.

Hippos have unique adaptations to their aquatic lifestyle, such as valves in their ears and nostrils that close when submerged to keep water out.

65.

Hippos are herbivores and primarily feed on grasses at night when they venture out of the water to graze.

66.

An adult hippo can consume up to 88 pounds (40 kg) of vegetation in a single night.

67.

Hippos have a complex social structure, with groups usually consisting of females and their offspring, led by a dominant male.

68.

Dominant males are highly territorial and mark their territory by spraying feces and urine using their spinning tail.

69.

Hippos use their tails not only for territorial marking but also as a rudder while swimming.

70.

Hippos have been observed engaging in playful behaviors, such as mock charging, splashing, and wrestling with each other.

71.

Hippos have been living on Earth for around 16 million years and have undergone relatively little change in their physical appearance during that time.

72.

Baby hippos are born underwater and weigh around 55-120 pounds (25-55 kg) at birth.

73.

Mother hippos are fiercely protective of their young and will keep them close, nursing them underwater.

74.

Despite their aquatic nature, hippos are not particularly buoyant and can walk along the bottom of rivers and lakes.

75.

Their dung plays a vital role in aquatic ecosystems, providing nutrients that support fish and other aquatic life.

76.

Hippos' closest living relatives are whales and porpoises, forming a group known as Cetancodonta.

77.

In Ancient Egyptian mythology, the god of fertility and water, Geb, was often depicted as a hippopotamus.

78.

Hippos' eyes, ears, and nostrils are situated at the top of their heads, allowing them to stay submerged while still being able to see, hear, and breathe.

79.

The lifespan of a hippo in the wild is around 40-50 years, while those in captivity can live longer.

80.

Their skin secretions have antibiotic properties that help protect them from infections and sunburns.

81.

Despite their size, hippos are surprisingly agile in water and can easily navigate through obstacles like fallen trees and rocks.

82.

Hippos have a prehensile upper lip that allows them to grasp and tear vegetation from the ground or trees.

83.

Hippos' sweat appears red when exposed to air due to the presence of a pigment called "hipposudoric acid."

84.

Their natural predators are crocodiles and, on occasion, lions and hyenas. However, adult hippos are formidable opponents even for these predators.

85.

Hippos often wallow in mud to keep their skin moisturized and to protect themselves from the sun.

86.

The hippopotamus has a four-chambered stomach that aids in digesting their plant-based diet.

87.

Hippos are depicted in various African tribal cultures, often associated with water, fertility, and protection.

88.

Hippos' dung is shaped like a mound, and they use their tails to spread it around to mark their territory.

89.

Hippos communicate through a variety of vocalizations, including grunts, snorts, and wheezes, which can be heard both underwater and on land.

90.

The decline of hippo populations is largely due to habitat loss and poaching for their ivory teeth and meat.

91.

In the wild, hippos spend most of their time submerged in water, as it provides them with protection from predators and the sun's heat.

92.

Hippos are not naturally aggressive towards humans but can become dangerous when feeling threatened or cornered.

93.

The collective noun for a group of hippos is a "bloat" or a "pod."

94.

The heart of a hippopotamus is large and can weigh up to 40 pounds (18 kg) or more.

95.

Hippos' eyes and ears are positioned high on their head, allowing them to remain submerged while still being aware of their surroundings.

96.

The population of hippos is decreasing due to habitat destruction and human encroachment into their natural habitats.

97.

In some African cultures, hippos are considered symbols of power, protection, and fertility, and their images are used in traditional art and jewelry.

98.

Hippos have an average body temperature of around 98.6°F (37°C), which helps them maintain their activity levels in both water and on land.

99.

Hippos' teeth are unique among mammals because they continue to grow throughout their lives. This adaptation helps compensate for the wear caused by their abrasive diet.

100.

Conservation efforts are critical to protect hippos and their habitats, as they play an important role in maintaining the balance of aquatic ecosystems.

101.

Sabino is a historic wooden passenger steamboat that was built in 1908.

102.

It is the oldest wooden, coal-fired steamboat still in operation in the United States.

103.

The Sabino was designed by renowned naval architect and marine engineer William Hand Jr.

104.

It was built by the Eastern Shipbuilding Company in New London, Connecticut.

105.

The Sabino is 57 feet (17 meters) in length and has a beam of 18 feet (5.5 meters).

106.

The steamboat's hull is made of white oak and yellow pine, and it features a distinctive raised pilot house.

107.

Sabino's original purpose was to transport passengers and freight between the Connecticut River towns of Deep River and East Haddam.

108.

It was named after an Indian chief of the Mohegan tribe, Chief Sowheag, whose name means "chief with a white head."

109.

The Sabino was used for various purposes over the years, including transportation, towing, and even as a floating warehouse.

110.

In 1974, the Sabino was designated a National Historic Landmark.

111.

The steam engine that powers the Sabino is a two-cylinder compound engine.

112.

Sabino's engine operates on coal, which is burned in the boiler to produce steam.

113.

The steam powers the engine's pistons, which turn the paddlewheel, propelling the boat through the water.

114.

The steamboat is well-known for its distinctive sound, which is a result of the rhythmic chuffing of its engine.

115.

Sabino was retired from commercial service in the 1960s but was later restored and returned to operation.

116.

It is now a popular attraction at the Mystic Seaport Museum in Mystic, Connecticut.

117.

The Sabino offers visitors a unique opportunity to experience a steam-powered vessel from the early 20th century.

118.

The steamboat operates daily during the museum's open season, providing visitors with short cruises on the Mystic River.

119.

The Sabino has retained much of its original appearance and features, making it an important artifact of maritime history.

120.

Restoration efforts included repairing the hull, replacing damaged components, and refurbishing the steam engine.

121.

Visitors can learn about the history of steam power, maritime transportation, and the Sabino's role in the region's history.

122.

Sabino's paddlewheel design, known as a "side-wheeler," is typical of steamboats from that era.

123.

The steamboat's upper deck features benches and seating for passengers to enjoy the river views.

124.

The Sabino's smokestack belches thick plumes of steam and smoke, creating an atmospheric scene.

125.

Steamboats like Sabino played a crucial role in the development of inland waterways as transportation routes.

126.

The Sabino's restoration was a collaborative effort involving skilled craftsmen, historians, and maritime enthusiasts.

127.

The steamboat has appeared in several films and documentaries, further solidifying its place in popular culture.

128.

Sabino's design is reminiscent of the golden age of steamboats that once plied American waterways.

129.

The boiler room is an essential part of the Sabino's operation, where coal is fed into the furnace to produce steam.

130.

The Sabino's restoration aimed to maintain its historical accuracy while ensuring it meets modern safety standards.

131.

The steamboat's regular cruises allow visitors to experience a piece of history while enjoying the scenic beauty of the Mystic River.

132.

The Sabino's appearance and operation provide a fascinating insight into the technology and craftsmanship of its time.

133.

The steamboat's paddlewheel is a marvel of engineering, efficiently propelling the vessel through the water.

134.

Sabino's return to service was celebrated by maritime enthusiasts and history buffs alike.

135.

The steamboat's distinctive red and white paint scheme reflects its classic and nostalgic appearance.

136.

Visitors have the opportunity to learn about the Sabino's history and significance through museum exhibits and guided tours.

137.

The Sabino's steam-powered operation requires careful maintenance and skilled engineers to keep it running smoothly.

138.

The steamboat's engine room is a captivating space filled with gleaming brass and polished metal components.

139.

The Sabino's operation provides a sensory experience, with the smell of coal and the rhythmic sound of the engine's chuffing.

140.

The steamboat's journey from commercial service to historical artifact highlights its enduring legacy.

141.

The Sabino has inspired generations of maritime enthusiasts, historians, and those interested in preserving cultural heritage.

142.

The steamboat's presence at the Mystic Seaport Museum contributes to the site's reputation as a premier maritime heritage destination.

143.

Sabino's role as an educational tool allows visitors to gain a deeper understanding of maritime history and technology.

144.

The steamboat's restoration project required extensive research to ensure historical accuracy in its design and features.

145.

The Sabino's connection to the Connecticut River region is an important aspect of its historical significance.

146.

Steamboats like Sabino contributed to the growth of tourism and recreation along America's waterways.

147.

The Sabino's return to operation was a labor of love, involving many individuals dedicated to preserving its legacy.

148.

The steamboat's paddlewheel generates a mesmerizing sight as it churns the water and propels the vessel forward.

149.

Sabino's iconic appearance and steam-powered operation evoke a sense of nostalgia for a bygone era of travel.

150.

The Sabino's ongoing operation and preservation serve as a testament to the importance of safeguarding maritime history for future generations.

151.

The Stanley-Whitman House is located in Farmington, Connecticut, and is one of the oldest houses in the state.

152.

It was built in 1720 by Benjamin and Anna Stanley and was later owned by the Whitman family.

153.

The house is an example of a "saltbox" style colonial home, characterized by its steep roof and lean-to structure.

154.

The Stanley-Whitman House is now a historic house museum that offers a glimpse into colonial life in New England.

155.

The museum features original furnishings, artifacts, and period-appropriate displays that showcase daily life in the 18th century.

156.

Visitors can explore the house's various rooms, including the kitchen, parlor, bedrooms, and study.

157.

The house's interior provides insights into early American architecture, design, and decorative arts.

158.

The Stanley-Whitman House is listed on the National Register of Historic Places.

159.

The property includes a barn, garden, and other outbuildings that reflect the agrarian lifestyle of the time.

160.

The museum offers guided tours, educational programs, and special events to engage visitors of all ages.

161.

The museum's staff and volunteers often dress in period clothing to enhance the historical experience for visitors.

162.

The Stanley-Whitman House is considered a valuable resource for historians and researchers studying colonial American life.

163.

The property underwent restoration and preservation efforts to ensure its historical accuracy and authenticity.

164.

The museum's garden features colonial-era plants and herbs, highlighting the importance of agriculture in early New England.

165.

The Stanley-Whitman House hosts workshops, lectures, and demonstrations that explore various aspects of colonial life.

166.

The museum's education programs cater to schools, offering students the chance to step back in time and learn about history hands-on.

167.

The site's colonial kitchen is often a focal point for demonstrations of traditional cooking methods and recipes.

168.

The house's original construction materials, such as wide floorboards and hand-hewn beams, showcase the craftsmanship of the time.

169.

The Stanley-Whitman House's location in Farmington provides insight into the town's history and development.

170.

The museum's collections include a wide range of artifacts, from textiles and ceramics to furniture and tools.

171.

The house's layout and furnishings reflect the social hierarchy and daily routines of colonial New England families.

172.

The museum's architecture and features make it an important example of early Connecticut domestic architecture.

173.

The Stanley-Whitman House often collaborates with other local historic sites and organizations to promote historical awareness.

174.

The museum's docents and interpreters provide engaging and informative tours that transport visitors back in time.

175.

The Stanley-Whitman House has been recognized for its efforts in preserving and interpreting New England's colonial history.

176.

The property's scenic surroundings help visitors imagine what life was like in a rural colonial community.

177.

The museum's exhibits delve into the stories of the families who lived in the house, revealing their challenges and aspirations.

178.

The Stanley-Whitman House offers visitors the chance to experience hands-on activities, such as hearth cooking and crafts.

179.

The site's educational programs align with state curriculum standards, making it a popular destination for school field trips.

180.

The Stanley-Whitman House's programs encourage visitors to ask questions, think critically, and engage with history in meaningful ways.

181.

The museum's location in a charming New England town adds to the overall experience of stepping back in time.

182.

The Stanley-Whitman House's architecture showcases the transition from early colonial homes to more refined Georgian-style residences.

183.

The museum's mission is not only to preserve the physical structure but also to tell the stories of the people who lived there.

184.

The Stanley-Whitman House's garden offers a peaceful retreat and a place for visitors to appreciate historical gardening practices.

185.

The site's interpretation of history extends beyond the house itself to encompass broader themes of colonial society.

186.

The museum's commitment to authenticity and accuracy ensures that visitors gain a true understanding of life in the 18th century.

187.

The Stanley-Whitman House's programs often incorporate period music, dance, and other forms of cultural expression.

188.

The site's proximity to other historic sites and attractions in Farmington makes it a popular destination for history enthusiasts.

189.

The museum's location within a historic district adds to its significance as a representation of early American life.

190.

The Stanley-Whitman House provides a unique perspective on the challenges and opportunities faced by colonial families.

191.

The site's educational initiatives extend beyond its physical grounds through outreach, workshops, and online resources.

192.

The museum's approach to interpretation emphasizes connections between the past and present, encouraging visitors to reflect on history's relevance.

193.

The Stanley-Whitman House serves as a hub for the local community, offering events and activities that foster a sense of belonging.

194.

The museum's exterior features classic colonial architectural elements, such as a central chimney and symmetrically placed windows.

195.

The Stanley-Whitman House has received recognition for its role in preserving and promoting New England's colonial heritage.

196.

The site's gardens showcase native plants and historically accurate gardening practices from the 18th century.

197.

The museum's volunteers and staff are passionate about history and dedicated to providing meaningful experiences for visitors.

198.

The Stanley-Whitman House's collections include a variety of objects that tell the stories of both the elite and working-class residents.

199.

The site's commitment to historical accuracy extends to details such as reproduction textiles, ceramics, and furniture.

200.

The Stanley-Whitman House invites visitors to explore the past and discover the interconnectedness of history, culture, and community.

201.

The Hobo Spider (Tegenaria agrestis) is a spider species native to Europe but has become established in the Pacific Northwest of the United States.

202.

It is commonly known as the "aggressive house spider" due to its often mistaken identity with the more dangerous brown recluse spider.

203.

Hobo spiders are medium-sized, typically ranging from 8 to 14 millimeters in body length.

204.

They have a distinctive chevron-shaped pattern on their abdomen, which can range from light tan to dark brown.

205.

Hobo spiders build funnel-shaped webs in dark and sheltered areas, such as basements, crawl spaces, and under rocks.

206.

Despite their intimidating appearance, hobo spiders are not considered aggressive towards humans and generally only bite if they feel threatened.

207.

Hobo spider bites are relatively rare and have been controversially associated with a condition called "necrotic arachnidism," where tissue necrosis can occur around the bite.

208.

The venom of the hobo spider contains toxins that can cause tissue damage, but its effects on humans are still debated among researchers.

209.

Hobo spiders are primarily nocturnal, hunting at night and resting during the day in their webs.

210.

They feed on insects that become trapped in their funnel-shaped webs.

211.

Hobo spiders are known for their characteristic zig-zag pattern of silk, known as a "stabilimentum," which they weave into their webs.

212.

The hobo spider's bite is often compared to that of a bee sting, with localized pain, redness, and swelling.

213.

Not all bites from hobo spiders result in tissue damage, and many go unnoticed due to mild or absent symptoms.

214.

The range of the hobo spider in the United States is mostly limited to the Pacific Northwest, including states like Washington, Oregon, Idaho, and Montana.

215.

Hobo spiders are often misidentified as brown recluse spiders due to their similar appearance, but they have distinct differences in their range and behavior.

216.

The hobo spider's scientific name, Tegenaria agrestis, is derived from the Latin word "agrestis," which means "of the fields."

217.

The hobo spider was first introduced to the United States in the early 20th century, likely through shipping and commerce.

218.

While the hobo spider's venom is being studied for its effects on human tissue, it also plays a role in immobilizing and digesting the spider's prey.

219.

Female hobo spiders have a longer lifespan than males, typically living for about two to three years, while males live for only a few months.

220.

Hobo spiders undergo a process called "molting," shedding their exoskeleton as they grow. They molt several times before reaching maturity.

221.

Males often enter homes in search of mates, which can lead to increased human encounters.

222.

The hobo spider's funnel-shaped web serves as both a trap for prey and a shelter for the spider.

223.

Hobo spiders are part of the larger family of funnel weaver spiders (Agelenidae), which are known for their distinct web-building behavior.

224.

Despite their name, hobo spiders are not known to hitch rides on trains or travel long distances like true hobos.

225.

The hobo spider's behavior and biology have been widely studied due to concerns about its potential medical significance.

226.

Some research suggests that the hobo spider's bite may not be as medically significant as once believed, and other factors may contribute to necrotic wounds.

227.

Hobo spiders are not typically found in densely populated urban areas but are more common in suburban and rural settings.

228.

Effective management of hobo spider populations can include sealing cracks and crevices in buildings and eliminating clutter that provides hiding places.

229.

Hobo spiders are not typically aggressive toward humans, and most bites occur when the spider is inadvertently provoked or trapped.

230.

Some individuals may have an allergic reaction to hobo spider bites, which can lead to more severe symptoms.

231.

Hobo spider populations tend to peak during the late summer and early fall months.

232.

The hobo spider's venom contains a mix of enzymes and toxins that aid in immobilizing and digesting prey.

233.

Despite concerns about their bite, hobo spiders are an essential part of ecosystems as predators of insects.

234.

The hobo spider's scientific classification places it in the Kingdom Animalia, Phylum Arthropoda, Class Arachnida, Order Araneae, and Family Agelenidae.

235.

While hobo spiders are not generally kept as pets, some people do keep them in captivity for study or educational purposes.

236.

The hobo spider's bite has been subject to urban legends and exaggerated reports, leading to misconceptions about its dangers.

237.

Hobo spiders are often confused with other common spiders, such as the giant house spider (Eratigena atrica).

238.

The best way to prevent hobo spider bites is to avoid handling or provoking spiders and taking precautions to keep them out of living spaces.

239.

Research into hobo spider venom continues to shed light on its composition and potential medical implications.

240.

The hobo spider's role in the ecosystem includes helping to control populations of other insects.

241.

While the hobo spider's venom can cause localized effects, such as redness and swelling, severe systemic reactions are extremely rare.

242.

Hobo spiders are more likely to bite if they feel cornered, threatened, or trapped against human skin or clothing.

243.

The hobo spider's reputation as a dangerous spider has led to significant research efforts to understand its biology and venom.

244.

Some regions with established hobo spider populations have developed educational programs to dispel myths and promote accurate information.

245.

The distinctive funnel-shaped webs of hobo spiders are often found in sheltered areas close to the ground, such as corners of buildings and sheds.

246.

Hobo spiders are skilled predators, using their webs to detect vibrations from potential prey and quickly capturing them.

247.

The hobo spider's bite can sometimes lead to an ulcerating wound that may take weeks to heal.

248.

Hobo spider populations can be managed by keeping indoor spaces clean and free of clutter that provides hiding places for the spiders.

249.

There is ongoing debate in the scientific community about the medical significance of hobo spider bites and their potential to cause necrotic wounds.

250.

Continued research into hobo spiders is essential to accurately understand their behavior, venom, and potential impact on humans.

251.

Honey bees belong to the genus Apis and are known for their vital role in pollination and honey production.

252.

There are several species of honey bees, with the most common being the European honey bee (Apis mellifera).

253.

Honey bees are social insects that live in colonies with a well-defined caste system: queens, workers, and drones.

254.

The queen bee is the largest member of the colony and is responsible for laying eggs. She can lay up to 2,000 eggs per day.

255.

Worker bees are female bees that perform various tasks, including foraging for food, caring for the young, and building the hive.

256.

Drones are male bees whose primary role is to mate with the queen. They are larger than worker bees but do not have stingers.

257.

Honey bees communicate through a complex dance language known as the "waggle dance," which conveys information about the location of food sources.

258.

Honey bees are known for their remarkable navigational skills, using the sun's position and landmarks to find their way back to the hive.

259.

Honey bees are critical pollinators for many crops, helping to ensure successful plant reproduction and food production.

260.

Honey bees are responsible for pollinating approximately one-third of the world's food crops.

261.

Honey bees collect nectar from flowers and store it in their honey stomach. Enzymes in the stomach begin the process of converting nectar into honey.

262.

Back at the hive, worker bees regurgitate and evaporate the nectar, transforming it into honey, which is then stored in the comb.

263.

Honey is not only a food source for honey bees but also serves as their primary source of energy during the winter months.

264.

Honey bees produce beeswax from glands on their abdomen. They use beeswax to build the hexagonal cells of the hive.

265.

The hexagonal shape of honeycomb cells maximizes storage space and structural strength in the hive.

266.

Honey bee colonies can consist of thousands of individual bees and are organized into a highly structured social order.

267.

Honey bees use propolis, a sticky resin collected from trees, to seal cracks and crevices in the hive, providing protection against pests and disease.

268.

Bees are excellent architects, constructing intricate hives with precise spacing and angles for optimal efficiency.

269.

Bees use pheromones to communicate and regulate behavior within the colony, helping to coordinate activities and maintain social cohesion.

270.

A colony's survival and success depend on a healthy queen, as her eggs are the foundation of the hive's workforce.

271.

The life cycle of a honey bee includes four stages: egg, larva, pupa, and adult. Different diets determine the bee's eventual role in the colony.

272.

Worker bees typically live for several weeks during the summer but can survive for several months during the winter.

273.

The average lifespan of a queen bee can range from one to three years, during which she can lay millions of eggs.

274.

Male drones have a relatively short life, living only a few weeks after mating or until the end of the mating season.

275.

Honey bees have a unique ability to regulate the temperature within the hive, ensuring the survival of the colony in various weather conditions.

276.

Honey bees use a technique called "swarming" to reproduce. A portion of the colony, including the old queen, leaves the hive to establish a new one.

277.

The process of swarming involves scout bees searching for suitable new nesting sites, such as tree hollows or crevices.

278.

Bees are masters of aerodynamics, using their wings to generate lift and hover in place, making them highly efficient pollinators.

279.

Bees have ultraviolet vision, allowing them to see patterns on flowers invisible to human eyes, guiding them to nectar-rich sources.

280.

Honey bees are known for their ability to fly up to 15 miles per hour, covering significant distances in search of food.

281.

A single honey bee can visit up to 2,000 flowers in a day, collecting nectar and pollen as they forage.

282.

Bees play a crucial role in maintaining biodiversity by pollinating plants that provide habitats and food for other species.

283.

Colony Collapse Disorder (CCD) is a phenomenon that has led to significant declines in honey bee populations. Its causes are still being studied, but factors like pesticides, habitat loss, and disease are thought to contribute.

284.

Honey bee populations are crucial for almond pollination in California, where nearly 80% of the world's almonds are grown.

285.

Honey bees are important to the global economy, contributing billions of dollars annually through pollination services and honey production.

286.

The practice of beekeeping, also known as apiculture, has been carried out for centuries, dating back to ancient civilizations.

287.

Beekeepers play a crucial role in supporting honey bee populations, managing hives, and ensuring their health and productivity.

288.

Bees are sensitive indicators of environmental health. Their population decline can signal broader ecological imbalances.

289.

The intricate dance of the honey bee and its role in pollination have inspired artists, scientists, and poets throughout history.

290.

Honey bee products, including honey, beeswax, royal jelly, and propolis, have been used for medicinal, cosmetic, and culinary purposes for centuries.

291.

Bees have inspired human technology, leading to innovations such as the development of hexagonal cell structures for construction and packaging.

292.

The ancient Egyptians considered honey to be a sacred food and used it in religious offerings and embalming.

293.

Honey bees have symbolic importance in various cultures, representing qualities like industriousness, community, and cooperation.

294.

Some species of bees engage in "nectar robbing," where they access nectar by puncturing the base of the flower without pollinating it.

295.

Honey bees have been studied for their ability to communicate about the quality and direction of food sources through the waggle dance.

296.

The role of honey bees in agriculture has gained renewed attention due to concerns about declining pollinator populations and their impact on food security.

297.

The "killer bee" or Africanized honey bee is a hybrid bee resulting from the crossbreeding of African and European honey bee subspecies. They are more aggressive and defensive than European honey bees.

298.

Honey bees have been studied for their ability to learn and remember complex tasks, such as navigating mazes to find food sources.

299.

Bees exhibit a behavior known as "cleaning house," where worker bees remove debris and dead bees from the hive to maintain hygiene.

300.

The study of honey bees, known as melittology, continues to reveal their fascinating behaviors, social structures, and ecological significance.

301.

Skechers is an American footwear brand founded in 1992 by Robert Greenberg in Manhattan Beach, California.

302.

The company originally started as a distributor of Doc Martens before transitioning to its own line of lifestyle and athletic footwear.

303.

The name "Skechers" was inspired by the term "skecher," which means "a person who sketches." This reflects the brand's creative and innovative approach to footwear design.

304.

The brand gained significant popularity in the mid-1990s with its trendy chunky sneakers known as "Skechers Energy" or "Skechers Sport."

305.

Skechers initially focused on casual and streetwear styles, but over the years, it expanded to include a wide range of footwear categories, including athletic, performance, and even dress shoes.

306.

In 1995, Skechers went public and began trading on the New York Stock Exchange under the symbol "SKX."

307.

Skechers' marketing campaigns have featured various celebrities over the years, including Britney Spears, Christina Aguilera, Kim Kardashian, and most notably, Joe Montana and Brooke Burke in the early 2000s.

308.

The brand's advertising catchphrase "It's the S" became well-known in the late 1990s and early 2000s.

309.

Skechers' global headquarters are located in Manhattan Beach, California, but the company has a strong international presence with distribution in over 170 countries.

310.

Skechers has collaborated with popular brands like Disney, One Piece, and even icons like The Beatles, resulting in unique and limited-edition footwear collections.

311.

In the early 2000s, Skechers expanded its product offerings to include children's shoes, performance footwear, and lifestyle sneakers.

312.

Skechers' performance division gained recognition with the launch of its innovative GOrun series, designed for running and training.

313.

The company has been involved in various philanthropic efforts, including partnerships with organizations like St. Jude Children's Research Hospital and Best Friends Animal Society.

314.

Skechers became known for its "S" logo, which often appears on the side of its shoes and has become synonymous with the brand's identity.

315.

The brand's tagline, "Skechers. Comfort Included," highlights its emphasis on providing comfortable footwear for various activities.

316.

Skechers' product range now includes not only footwear but also apparel and accessories like bags and socks.

317.

In 2010, Skechers introduced its Shape-Ups line, which claimed to provide health and fitness benefits through its unique sole design. The shoes were met with both popularity and controversy.

318.

The company faced lawsuits related to its Shape-Ups line, with claims that the shoes' health benefits were misleading or unproven.

319.

Despite the controversies, Skechers remains one of the leading athletic and lifestyle footwear brands globally.

320.

Skechers has received awards for its innovative footwear technologies, such as its memory foam cushioning and lightweight materials.

321.

The brand has also expanded its retail presence, with standalone Skechers stores and partnerships with other retailers to offer its products.

322.

In 2018, Skechers launched its D'Lites line, a modern take on its iconic chunky sneakers from the 1990s.

323.

Skechers has a focus on sustainability and has made efforts to incorporate eco-friendly materials and practices into its production processes.

324.

The company has gained recognition for its performance footwear worn by professional athletes in various sports, including running, golf, and baseball.

325.

Skechers often sponsors sporting events and athletes, contributing to its visibility and association with sports culture.

326.

Skechers' marketing campaigns have evolved over the years, with a shift toward highlighting athletes' stories and achievements.

327.

The brand's product offerings include a wide range of styles for men, women, and children, catering to various tastes and preferences.

328.

In recent years, Skechers has also introduced technology-focused footwear, such as its arch support and air-cooled memory foam designs.

329.

Skechers has been ranked as one of the top athletic and casual footwear brands in the United States, competing with established giants like Nike and Adidas.

330.

The brand's success is attributed to its ability to adapt to changing fashion trends while maintaining a strong commitment to comfort and quality.

331.

Skechers' success in the footwear market has led it to venture into other product categories, including eyewear, watches, and backpacks.

332.

Skechers' stock price has experienced fluctuations over the years, influenced by factors such as market trends, product launches, and economic conditions.

333.

Skechers has a strong online presence, offering its products through its official website and various e-commerce platforms.

334.

The brand's international expansion has included opening flagship stores in major cities around the world.

335.

Skechers has a history of supporting charitable causes, including disaster relief efforts and educational initiatives.

336.

The brand's commitment to innovation is evident in its continuous development of new technologies and materials for its footwear.

337.

Skechers has been recognized with various industry awards for its innovative designs and contributions to the footwear industry.

338.

The company's diverse product range caters to a wide demographic, from active individuals to those seeking casual and stylish options.

339.

Skechers' advertising campaigns often focus on its core values of comfort, style, and versatility.

340.

Skechers' global reach and popularity have made it a recognizable brand in both developed and emerging markets.

341.

The brand's success story showcases the significance of adapting to changing consumer preferences and technological advancements.

342.

Skechers has embraced digital marketing and social media platforms to engage with its customers and promote its products.

343.

The company's revenue growth over the years has solidified its position as a major player in the footwear industry.

344.

Skechers has consistently invested in research and development to enhance the performance and comfort of its footwear.

345.

The brand's collaborations with celebrities and designers have led to limited-edition collections that generate excitement among consumers.

346.

Skechers' commitment to sustainability includes efforts to reduce its carbon footprint and use recycled materials in its products.

347.

The brand has a dedicated customer base that appreciates its combination of style and comfort.

348.

Skechers has faced competition from both traditional athletic footwear brands and newer entrants in the market.

349.

The company's partnerships with athletes and fitness influencers have contributed to its credibility in the performance footwear category.

350.

Skechers' enduring popularity is a testament to its ability to resonate with a diverse range of consumers and remain relevant in a competitive industry.

351.

Paychex was founded in 1971 by Tom Golisano in Rochester, New York, with an initial investment of just $3,000.

352.

The company's name "Paychex" is derived from "pay" and "checks," reflecting its focus on payroll processing.

353.

Paychex initially started as a small business offering payroll processing services to local companies.

354.

Tom Golisano started Paychex with the goal of providing small businesses with an affordable and efficient solution for managing payroll and human resources.

355.

The company's first office was in the basement of a building in Rochester.

356.

In its early days, Paychex relied on manual processes, including handwritten paychecks.

357.

Paychex's first computerized payroll processing system was developed in 1979.

358.

The company went public in 1983, trading on the NASDAQ stock exchange under the ticker symbol "PAYX."

359.

Paychex expanded its services beyond payroll to include other human resource-related solutions, such as benefits administration and retirement planning.

360.

The 1990s saw significant growth for Paychex as it introduced new technology-driven solutions and expanded its customer base.

361.

In 1999, Paychex introduced its first web-based payroll system, allowing clients to access their payroll data online.

362.

The company's growth was fueled by its commitment to customer service and its focus on meeting the needs of small and medium-sized businesses.

363.

Paychex acquired several other payroll and HR companies in the 1990s and 2000s, expanding its market presence.

364.

In 2004, Paychex introduced the "Paychex Online Payroll" platform, which allowed businesses to process payroll entirely online.

365.

Paychex further expanded its service offerings to include time and attendance tracking, employee screening, and HR consulting.

366.

The company's commitment to innovation led to the development of mobile apps for clients to manage payroll and HR tasks on the go.

367.

Paychex introduced a comprehensive suite of cloud-based human capital management (HCM) solutions to address the evolving needs of businesses.

368.

In 2019, Paychex celebrated its 100th location, highlighting its nationwide presence.

369.

Paychex has consistently been ranked among the top payroll and HR outsourcing providers in the United States.

370.

The company has received numerous awards for its workplace culture and commitment to employee satisfaction.

371.

Paychex launched its "Flex" time and attendance solution, allowing employees to clock in and out using mobile devices or biometric terminals.

372.

The company's growth extended beyond the United States, with operations in Europe and other international markets.

373.

Paychex acquired several other HR technology and service companies to enhance its offerings and provide end-to-end solutions.

374.

The company's expansion into the PEO (Professional Employer Organization) industry allowed it to offer comprehensive HR solutions for businesses of all sizes.

375.

Paychex's "Human Resource Services" division provides businesses with HR outsourcing, employee handbooks, and compliance assistance.

376.

The company's "Retirement Services" division offers retirement plan administration and record-keeping services for businesses.

377.

Paychex has been recognized for its commitment to corporate social responsibility and charitable initiatives.

378.

The company offers educational resources, webinars, and workshops to help businesses stay informed about changing regulations and best practices.

379.

Paychex provides support for businesses navigating the complex world of healthcare compliance and benefits administration.

380.

The company's commitment to data security and privacy is reflected in its stringent measures to protect client information.

381.

Paychex's cloud-based solutions enable businesses to access and manage payroll and HR data from anywhere with an internet connection.

382.

In 2020, Paychex launched "Paychex Promise," a commitment to providing the best customer experience in the industry.

383.

The company's "MyPaychex" portal allows employees to access their pay stubs, tax forms, and other important documents online.

384.

Paychex has adapted to changing work trends by offering solutions for remote work, flexible scheduling, and hybrid work environments.

385.

The company's CEO, Martin Mucci, has been recognized for his leadership and contributions to the payroll and HR industry.

386.

Paychex has been featured in various business publications and media outlets for its innovative solutions and industry insights.

387.

The company's commitment to diversity and inclusion is reflected in its workforce and corporate initiatives.

388.

Paychex's growth strategy includes partnerships with other industry leaders to enhance its product offerings and expand its reach.

389.

The company's quarterly "Pulse of HR" survey provides insights into HR trends and challenges facing businesses.

390.

Paychex has a significant presence in the professional sports industry, providing payroll and HR services for sports teams and athletes.

391.

The company's commitment to customer service includes a dedicated team of specialists available to assist clients with their needs.

392.

Paychex has won numerous awards for its technological advancements, customer service, and workplace culture.

393.

The company's blog and resource center offer valuable insights into payroll, HR, and business management topics.

394.

Paychex's "Flex Time" feature allows employees to manage their schedules and request time off through an online portal.

395.

The company's "Paychex Flex" platform is designed to scale with businesses as they grow and evolve.

396.

Paychex has a strong presence in the nonprofit sector, providing tailored solutions for organizations with unique needs.

397.

The company's commitment to education includes offering a range of training resources for clients to optimize their use of Paychex solutions.

398.

Paychex's philanthropic efforts extend to scholarships, disaster relief support, and community engagement initiatives.

399.

The company's "Wage-on-Demand" feature allows employees to access their earned wages ahead of traditional payday.

400.

Paychex continues to evolve its offerings to meet the changing needs of businesses, supporting them with cutting-edge technology and expertise in payroll, HR, and benefits administration.

401.

The Steward's House was part of the Foreign Mission School, a historic institution in Cornwall, Connecticut, established in the early 19th century.

402.

The Foreign Mission School aimed to train young men from indigenous cultures and distant lands to become Christian missionaries.

403.

The Steward's House served as the residence for the school's steward, who managed the day-to-day operations and provisions of the school.

404.

The Foreign Mission School was founded in 1816 by the American Board of Commissioners for Foreign Missions (ABCFM).

405.

The Steward's House, built in 1817, is a fine example of Federal architecture and has been well-preserved over the centuries.

406.

The building's architecture features elegant Georgian and Federal-style elements, including its symmetry and balanced design.

407.

The Steward's House is characterized by its two-and-a-half-story structure, gabled roof, and double chimneys.

408.

The school's primary focus was to educate young men from non-Christian backgrounds to become missionaries and spread Christianity.

409.

The students at the Foreign Mission School came from various countries, including the Hawaiian Islands, India, China, and Native American tribes.

410.

Many of the students at the school were taught to read and write in English, along with receiving religious education.

411.

The Steward's House served as a communal living space for students who lived, studied, and worked together in a controlled environment.

412.

The school aimed to bridge cultural divides and convert students to Christianity, which often led to the loss of their original cultural practices.

413.

Notable students from the school included Henry ʻŌpūkahaʻia, a Hawaiian who played a pivotal role in the Christianization of Hawaii.

414.

The school operated until 1826, after which it faced financial challenges and eventually closed its doors.

415.

Following its closure, the Steward's House underwent various uses, including serving as a boarding house and private residence.

416.

The building's historical significance led to its recognition as a National Historic Landmark in 1960.

417.

In 2001, the Foreign Mission School site, including the Steward's House, was designated as a National Historic Landmark District.

418.

The Cornwall Historical Society acquired the Steward's House in 1954 and worked to restore and preserve the historic structure.

419.

The Steward's House now serves as a museum and interpretive center, offering insights into the history of the Foreign Mission School.

420.

The museum showcases artifacts, documents, and exhibits that tell the story of the students, the school's mission, and its impact.

421.

The Steward's House stands as a reminder of the complex intersections of culture, religion, and education in the early 19th century.

422.

The site is a valuable educational resource for understanding the historical context of missionary efforts during that era.

423.

The Foreign Mission School's history reflects broader themes of colonialism, cultural exchange, and the spread of Christianity.

424.

The Steward's House and the Foreign Mission School site continue to host educational programs and events for visitors.

425.

The Steward's House is located in the scenic town of Cornwall, Connecticut, surrounded by picturesque landscapes.

426.

The restoration of the Steward's House aimed to preserve its original architectural features while making it accessible to the public.

427.

The museum's exhibits provide perspectives on the experiences of the students and the challenges they faced in adapting to a new culture.

428.

The Steward's House and the Foreign Mission School highlight the complexities of cross-cultural interactions and their lasting impact.

429.

The museum's interpretation encourages visitors to reflect on the historical legacy of missionary activities and their implications.

430.

The Steward's House is part of a network of historic sites that shed light on the social, cultural, and religious history of the United States.

431.

The Cornwall Historical Society works diligently to maintain the authenticity and historical accuracy of the Steward's House.

432.

The museum offers guided tours, lectures, and workshops that delve into the history of the Foreign Mission School.

433.

The Steward's House has been featured in documentaries and publications that explore the history of mission schools and their effects.

434.

The museum's exhibits explore the experiences of students who traveled great distances to learn in a foreign environment.

435.

The Steward's House serves as a site for reflection on the complex interplay between faith, education, and cultural identity.

436.

The National Historic Landmark District designation underscores the historical and cultural significance of the Foreign Mission School site.

437.

The museum's dedication to scholarship and historical accuracy contributes to a deeper understanding of the Foreign Mission School's legacy.

438.

The Steward's House offers visitors a chance to step back in time and experience the physical environment where students lived and learned.

439.

The museum fosters discussions about cultural appropriation, religious conversion, and the preservation of indigenous identities.

440.

The story of the Foreign Mission School serves as a lens through which to examine the broader history of American missionary movements.

441.

The Steward's House and the Foreign Mission School highlight the efforts of early American missionaries to engage with diverse cultures.

442.

The building's architectural features reflect the craftsmanship of the early 19th century and the historical context in which it was built.

443.

The Steward's House is a testament to the Cornwall Historical Society's commitment to preserving and sharing local history.

444.

The site's guided tours provide insights into the daily lives of students who called the Steward's House home.

445.

The museum engages with contemporary discussions about cultural sensitivity, religious pluralism, and historical representation.

446.

The Steward's House's restoration aimed to maintain its historical integrity while adapting it for modern educational purposes.

447.

The museum's exhibits challenge visitors to consider the complexities of cultural exchange and the role of education in shaping identities.

448.

The Cornwall Historical Society's dedication to the Steward's House reflects a broader effort to celebrate the town's history.

449.

The museum offers visitors a glimpse into the challenges and opportunities faced by the students who attended the Foreign Mission School.

450.

The Steward's House continues to be a valuable resource for understanding the multifaceted history of cross-cultural interactions and the quest for education and understanding.

451.

The Harriet Beecher Stowe House is located in Cincinnati, Ohio, and is the former residence of Harriet Beecher Stowe, author of the influential anti-slavery novel "Uncle Tom's Cabin."

452.

The house is a National Historic Landmark and has become a museum dedicated to preserving the legacy of Harriet Beecher Stowe and her contributions to American literature and social justice.

453.

Harriet Beecher Stowe wrote "Uncle Tom's Cabin" in this house, which was published in 1852 and played a significant role in shaping public opinion about slavery and the abolitionist movement.

454.

The house was built in 1832 and reflects the Federal architectural style of the time with its red brick exterior and symmetrical design.

455.

The Stowe House is open to the public for guided tours, allowing visitors to explore the rooms where Harriet Beecher Stowe lived and wrote.

456.

The house showcases period furnishings and artifacts that provide insight into the daily life and work of the Stowe family.

457.

Harriet Beecher Stowe's father, Lyman Beecher, was a prominent Congregationalist minister, and her sister Catharine Beecher was an advocate for women's education.

458.

The Stowe House offers exhibits that delve into the history of the Beecher family, including their contributions to social reform and education.

459.

The house's location in Cincinnati was strategic, as it was situated on the border between the free Northern states and the slave-holding Southern states.

460.

Harriet Beecher Stowe was inspired to write "Uncle Tom's Cabin" after her experiences interacting with escaped slaves and hearing their stories in Cincinnati.

461.

"Uncle Tom's Cabin" had a profound impact on public sentiment and contributed to the abolitionist movement, eventually leading to the Civil War.

462.

The house is not only a literary landmark but also a site of historical significance in the fight against slavery and racial injustice.

463.

The Stowe House is part of the Harriet Beecher Stowe House and Research Center, which offers educational programs and events for visitors.

464.

The museum's exhibits highlight the connections between Harriet Beecher Stowe's writing and the broader social and political context of her time.

465.

Harriet Beecher Stowe's advocacy extended beyond slavery; she also supported women's rights, temperance, and other social reform movements.

466.

The Stowe House underwent restoration efforts to preserve its historical integrity and provide an immersive experience for visitors.

467.

The house's library contains a collection of books and resources related to Harriet Beecher Stowe, her works, and the era in which she lived.

468.

The museum's programming includes lectures, workshops, and discussions about the lasting impact of "Uncle Tom's Cabin."

469.

The Harriet Beecher Stowe House is a place for reflection on the power of literature to effect social change and promote empathy.

470.

The house is an example of how individual voices and actions can contribute to transformative societal shifts.

471.

Visitors can explore the various rooms of the house, including the study where Harriet Beecher Stowe wrote many of her works.

472.

The Stowe House's significance goes beyond the local community; it is recognized as a site of national historical importance.

473.

The museum collaborates with educational institutions and organizations to promote scholarship related to Harriet Beecher Stowe and her impact.

474.

The Stowe House's exhibits encourage dialogue about race, equality, and justice, making it a relevant and engaging destination for all ages.

475.

The location of the house provides context for understanding the complex history of the Underground Railroad and the struggle for freedom.

476.

The Stowe House stands as a tribute to Harriet Beecher Stowe's dedication to social justice and her belief in the power of storytelling.

477.

The house offers insights into Harriet Beecher Stowe's personal life, including her relationships with family members and fellow reformers.

478.

The Stowe House connects Harriet Beecher Stowe's Cincinnati experiences with her later life in Maine and her continued advocacy.

479.

The museum's guided tours provide historical context and allow visitors to ask questions and engage with the exhibits.

480.

The Harriet Beecher Stowe House has received accolades and recognition for its educational programs and preservation efforts.

481.

The house serves as a reminder that literature can serve as a catalyst for change and inspire social activism.

482.

The Stowe House welcomes visitors from all backgrounds to explore the life and work of Harriet Beecher Stowe and the issues she championed.

483.

The museum's exhibits shed light on the challenges and prejudices faced by Harriet Beecher Stowe as a female author and activist.

484.

The Stowe House's commitment to preserving and sharing history contributes to a deeper understanding of America's struggle for equality.

485.

The house's proximity to the Ohio River serves as a tangible reminder of the historic role the river played in the Underground Railroad.

486.

The Stowe House's location in the historic Walnut Hills neighborhood adds to its charm and connection to the local community.

487.

The museum's outreach efforts extend beyond its physical location, engaging with digital audiences and fostering ongoing discussions.

488.

The Stowe House's archives hold a wealth of primary sources, letters, and documents related to Harriet Beecher Stowe's life and work.

489.

The house is a place of inspiration for aspiring writers, activists, and advocates who seek to make a positive impact on society.

490.

The Stowe House continues to be a place where individuals can learn about the power of storytelling and its role in shaping history.

491.

The museum's educational initiatives aim to empower visitors to confront issues of injustice and promote empathy and understanding.

492.

The Stowe House's educational programs cater to students of all ages, promoting critical thinking and historical awareness.

493.

The house offers visitors a glimpse into the domestic life of Harriet Beecher Stowe and her family through carefully preserved artifacts.

494.

The Stowe House's dedication to historical accuracy and research ensures that its exhibits reflect the most current scholarship.

495.

The museum provides resources for teachers and educators to incorporate Harriet Beecher Stowe's legacy into their curriculum.

496.

The house's engagement with contemporary issues makes it a relevant and thought-provoking destination for today's visitors.

497.

The Stowe House's commitment to inclusivity and accessibility ensures that its exhibits and programs are available to diverse audiences.

498.

The museum's role in the preservation of literary and social history underscores the importance of valuing and protecting cultural heritage.

499.

The Stowe House encourages visitors to consider the impact of their own actions and choices on society and future generations.

500.

The museum's ongoing efforts to celebrate Harriet Beecher Stowe's contributions ensure that her legacy continues to inspire positive change.

501.

The hoopoe (Upupa epops) is a striking and distinctive bird known for its unique appearance and behavior.

502.

Hoopoes are found across Europe, Asia, and parts of Africa, with their range extending from temperate to tropical regions.

503.

The name "hoopoe" is derived from its distinctive call, which sounds like "hoo-poo" or "hoo-poo-poo."

504.

These birds are about the size of a dove, measuring around 25-32 centimeters (10-12.5 inches) in length.

505.

The hoopoe has a distinctive crown of feathers on its head that it can raise or lower, depending on its mood.

506.

The hoopoe's plumage is a combination of pink, orange, and black, with striking black and white striped wings.

507.

They have a long, slender bill adapted for probing and extracting insects from the ground.

508.

Hoopoes are known for their bold and confident demeanor, often walking or hopping with a distinctive upright posture.

509.

These birds are highly migratory, with some populations traveling long distances during seasonal migrations.

510.

Hoopoes are cavity nesters and often utilize tree hollows or crevices in rocks for nesting sites.

511.

They line their nests with softer materials like leaves, feathers, and grass.

512.

Female hoopoes typically lay around 3-6 eggs per clutch, and both parents take turns incubating them.

513.

The hoopoe's diet primarily consists of insects, worms, and other invertebrates found in the soil.

514.

They use their long bills to probe the ground for food, and their specialized bills can detect movement underground.

515.

Hoopoes have a mutualistic relationship with certain animals like mammals and herbivorous birds. These animals follow the hoopoes to feed on insects they disturb.

516.

Hoopoes are often associated with ancient symbolism and are mentioned in various mythologies and religious texts.

517.

In Ancient Egyptian culture, the hoopoe was associated with the sun god Ra and was considered a symbol of protection.

518.

The hoopoe appears in the Bible as a creature with unclean habits due to its diet, mentioned in Leviticus 11:13-19.

519.

In many cultures, the hoopoe is considered a symbol of happiness, good luck, and resurrection.

520.

Their distinctive appearance has made hoopoes popular subjects in folklore, art, and literature.

521.

The hoopoe's unique crown of feathers plays a role in courtship displays, with males raising their crowns as part of their mating rituals.

522.

These birds are known for their strong territorial behavior, defending their nesting sites vigorously.

523.

Hoopoes have a specialized preen gland near the base of their tail that produces an oily substance used for grooming their feathers.

524.

Despite their striking appearance, hoopoes can be quite inconspicuous in their natural habitat due to their cryptic coloration.

525.

Hoopoes have a wide range of vocalizations, including calls, trills, and hisses, which they use to communicate with each other.

526.

In some cultures, the hoopoe's call is believed to signify the arrival of rain, making it a symbol of hope for farmers.

527.

Hoopoes are known to engage in sunbathing, spreading their wings and exposing their plumage to the sun to help rid themselves of parasites.

528.

These birds have been studied for their fascinating migratory patterns, navigation abilities, and social behaviors.

529.

The hoopoe's flight is characterized by strong, direct wing beats interspersed with gliding.

530.

In Pakistan, the hoopoe is considered the national bird and is known as the "Hudhud."

531.

The hoopoe is the state bird of Israel and holds cultural significance in Middle Eastern and North African countries.

532.

In Islamic tradition, the hoopoe is mentioned in the story of King Solomon's encounter with the bird, highlighting its intelligence.

533.

Hoopoes are capable of remarkable feats of endurance during their migratory journeys, covering vast distances.

534.

These birds face threats from habitat loss, pollution, and changes in agricultural practices that impact their food sources.

535.

Hoopoes have been depicted in ancient Egyptian hieroglyphs and artwork, showcasing their long-standing cultural significance.

536.

The hoopoe's unique appearance has earned it the nickname "crowned bird" or "crowned hoopoe."

537.

Their ability to dig for insects and larvae in the soil contributes to controlling pest populations in their ecosystems.

538.

Hoopoes have been known to defend their nests aggressively against larger birds, such as crows and magpies.

539.

The hoopoe's long bill allows it to extract insects from crevices and cracks that other birds might not be able to reach.

540.

Hoopoes are monogamous during the breeding season, forming strong pair bonds to raise their offspring.

541.

The hoopoe has a relatively short lifespan in the wild, averaging around 5-6 years.

542.

These birds are known to migrate across the Himalayas, one of the world's most challenging mountain ranges.

543.

The hoopoe's bold and colorful appearance is thought to serve as a warning signal to predators that it may be unpalatable or harmful.

544.

Hoopoes are an important component of various ecosystems, contributing to nutrient cycling through their feeding behavior.

545.

They play a role in seed dispersal as they consume fruits and disperse the seeds in their feces.

546.

In some cultures, the hoopoe is believed to have healing and protective powers, leading to its use in traditional medicine and rituals.

547.

The hoopoe's conservation status varies among different regions, with some populations facing more significant threats than others.

548.

Conservation efforts are being undertaken to protect the habitats of hoopoes and raise awareness about their ecological importance.

549.

The hoopoe's ability to thrive in diverse habitats, from urban areas to woodlands, showcases its adaptability as a species.

550.

Hoopoes continue to captivate the imagination of people worldwide, contributing to their status as a beloved and iconic bird species.

551.

Hornets are a type of large wasp, belonging to the genus Vespa, and are known for their distinct appearance and behavior.

552.

There are various species of hornets found around the world, with the most well-known being the European hornet (Vespa crabro).

553.

Hornets are larger than common wasps and bees, with adults ranging from 0.75 to 2.2 inches (19 to 55 mm) in length.

554.

Their bodies are typically black, brown, or reddish-brown, and they have yellow markings on their abdomen and head.

555.

Hornets are social insects and live in colonies, with a caste system consisting of queens, workers, and males.

556.

The queen hornet is the largest individual in the colony and is responsible for laying eggs and establishing and maintaining the nest.

557.

The workers, which are sterile females, perform various tasks such as foraging for food, caring for the young, and defending the colony.

558.

Male hornets, also known as drones, are responsible for mating with the queen and do not have a stinger.

559.

Hornets build nests from a paper-like material they create by chewing wood and mixing it with their saliva.

560.

Nests are usually built in sheltered locations like tree hollows, attics, or wall voids.

561.

Hornets' nests are often constructed in layers of hexagonal cells, and each cell serves as a chamber for developing hornet larvae.

562.

The workers diligently care for the developing larvae, feeding them a diet of chewed-up insects and nectar.

563.

Hornets are predatory insects and are known for their hunting abilities. They primarily feed on other insects, including bees, flies, and caterpillars.

564.

Hornets are equipped with powerful mandibles that allow them to chew through tough insect exoskeletons.

565.

Unlike some other wasp species, hornets are less likely to scavenge for human food and are not as attracted to sweet substances.

566.

Hornets are known for their painful stings, which can be especially dangerous for those with allergies.

567.

The hornet's sting delivers a potent venom that can cause localized pain, swelling, and even systemic reactions in sensitive individuals.

568.

Hornets release pheromones to communicate with each other. Alarm pheromones can trigger defensive behaviors, and other pheromones help mark foraging paths and locate food sources.

569.

Hornets are also beneficial insects as they help control pest populations, particularly harmful insects that can damage crops or gardens.

570.

In some Asian cultures, hornet larvae and pupae are considered delicacies and are consumed as food.

571.

Hornets are known for their impressive flight capabilities, including high speeds and agile maneuvers.

572.

The buzzing sound produced by a hornet in flight comes from the rapid beating of its wings.

573.

Hornets are more active during the daytime and tend to rest at night.

574.

While hornets are generally not aggressive, they will defend their nest if they feel it is threatened.

575.

The lifespan of hornets varies depending on the species, with worker hornets living several weeks and queens surviving through the winter to establish new colonies.

576.

Hornets are found in various habitats, including forests, woodlands, meadows, and urban areas.

577.

Some hornet species, like the Asian giant hornet (Vespa mandarinia), are known for their impressive size, with queens reaching up to 2.5 inches (63 mm) in length.

578.

The Asian giant hornet is the largest hornet species in the world and has a fearsome reputation due to its size and potentially lethal sting.

579.

Hornets are known for their complex nesting behaviors and architectural skills, creating intricate structures that can include multiple combs and layers.

580.

Hornets have specialized hairs on their bodies that help collect pollen, which they use as a protein source to feed their larvae.

581.

Hornets are sensitive to changes in temperature and weather conditions, and their behavior can vary based on environmental factors.

582.

In some cultures, hornets have symbolic meanings, representing everything from courage and strength to danger and chaos.

583.

The venom from hornet stings has been studied for its potential medical applications, including pain relief and cancer treatment.

584.

Hornets are known for their ability to emit a clicking sound by rapidly snapping their mandibles together, which is often used as a warning signal to potential threats.

585.

Hornets are attracted to bright colors, sugary substances, and strong scents, which can inadvertently draw them to human activities.

586.

In the wild, hornets help pollinate flowers as they collect nectar for themselves and food for their young.

587.

Hornets have a limited lifespan, and their colonies typically last for only one season.

588.

Some hornet species engage in a behavior known as "hilltopping," where they gather at high points in their environment to mate.

589.

Hornets have been used in scientific research to study their behavior, communication, and navigation abilities.

590.

Hornets are part of the ecosystem, providing food for predators such as birds, spiders, and other insects.

591.

The introduction of invasive hornet species in certain regions can have detrimental effects on native ecosystems and local insect populations.

592.

Hornets have been used in traditional medicine in some cultures, although their venom can be harmful if not properly administered.

593.

Hornets are related to other social wasps, such as yellow jackets and paper wasps, and share similar behaviors and characteristics.

594.

Hornets can travel several miles in search of food, making them important pollinators over larger distances.

595.

The European hornet is one of the few hornet species found in North America, having been introduced by settlers from Europe.

596.

Hornets are known for their distinctive flight pattern, which includes rapid, darting movements as they navigate through their environment.

597.

Hornets are an integral part of ecosystems as they help control insect populations, preventing overpopulation and pest outbreaks.

598.

Some hornet species, like the European hornet, are less likely to sting humans unless provoked, and they often avoid contact.

599.

Hornets have been depicted in various forms of art and literature throughout history, symbolizing different cultural meanings and interpretations.

600.

Hornets continue to capture the curiosity of researchers and nature enthusiasts, offering insights into the fascinating world of insects and their roles in the environment.

601.

The Dow Chemical Company was founded on May 17, 1897, by Herbert H. Dow in Midland, Michigan, USA.

602.

Dow's initial focus was on extracting bromine from brine in the Midland region, which had numerous applications, including photographic chemicals and medicines.

603.

Herbert H. Dow's pioneering work in chemical extraction led to the development of the Dow Process, a method for extracting bromine from brine.

604.

The company's first plant, known as the "Bromine Works," began operation in 1898, marking the official start of Dow Chemical.

605.

Dow played a crucial role in World War I by producing materials such as phenol for explosives and chlorine for disinfection.

606.

In 1930, Dow introduced the world's first commercially available synthetic resin called Styron, which laid the foundation for modern plastics.

607.

Dow was one of the key contributors to the Manhattan Project during World War II, producing materials for the atomic bomb.

608.

After the war, Dow diversified its product range to include agricultural chemicals, plastics, and consumer goods.

609.

The 1950s marked the development of Dow's polyethylene plastic, which revolutionized packaging and manufacturing.

610.

Dow's innovative silicone technology was used to create the world's first silicone breast implant in the 1960s.

611.

In 1973, Dow introduced the Dow Corning brand for its silicone-based products, including adhesives, sealants, and medical applications.

612.

The company expanded internationally in the 1970s, opening facilities in various countries to serve global markets.

613.

Dow was one of the first companies to invest in sustainability efforts, establishing its Environmental Affairs Division in 1971.

614.

The 1980s saw Dow's involvement in developing products like solar cells and antifreeze.

615.

Dow's acquisition of Union Carbide Corporation in 2001 expanded its product portfolio and global reach.

616.

Dow was among the first companies to develop technology for the production of bio-based plastics from renewable resources.

617.

The company launched the "Human Element" brand campaign in 2006 to highlight its commitment to science and innovation.

618.

Dow Chemical and DuPont announced a merger in 2015, forming DowDuPont Inc., which later split into three separate companies.

619.

In 2019, Dow Inc. became a standalone company once again, focusing on materials science and chemical manufacturing.

620.

Dow has been recognized for its sustainability efforts, including being named to the Dow Jones Sustainability Index multiple times.

621.

The company has actively worked to reduce its environmental footprint through initiatives like energy efficiency and waste reduction.

622.

Dow's innovations have led to products used in everyday life, from food packaging and electronics to construction materials.

623.

The company has a history of collaborating with other businesses, research institutions, and governments to address global challenges.

624.

Dow has received numerous awards for its commitment to diversity and inclusion in the workplace.

625.

Dow has made significant contributions to water conservation and has set ambitious goals to address water scarcity.

626.

The company's research efforts have led to advancements in chemistry, material science, and sustainable technologies.

627.

Dow's solutions have been integral in addressing challenges like climate change, clean water access, and renewable energy.

628.

Dow has a strong commitment to safety, investing in technologies and practices to protect its workforce and communities.

629.

Dow's Midland, Michigan headquarters is home to the Dow Diamond, a minor league baseball stadium and community gathering space.

630.

The company is a leader in developing advanced materials for the automotive industry, enabling lighter and more fuel-efficient vehicles.

631.

Dow has expanded its product range to include advanced electronics materials used in devices like smartphones and wearables.

632.

The company's innovative packaging solutions help reduce food waste and improve product shelf life.

633.

Dow has a history of supporting STEM education initiatives to inspire the next generation of scientists and engineers.

634.

Dow's commitment to innovation is reflected in its extensive portfolio of patents and intellectual property.

635.

The company has been recognized for its corporate social responsibility efforts and charitable contributions.

636.

Dow's global operations encompass a wide range of industries, including agriculture, consumer goods, infrastructure, and more.

637.

Dow has a strong focus on reducing greenhouse gas emissions and has set targets to achieve net-zero carbon emissions.

638.

The company's research efforts have led to advancements in polymer science, enabling the development of new materials.

639.

Dow's commitment to sustainability extends to its product life cycle, from raw material sourcing to end-of-life recycling.

640.

Dow has played a role in shaping chemical industry regulations and standards globally.

641.

The company's commitment to safety and operational excellence has earned it numerous awards and recognitions.

642.

Dow has a history of philanthropic initiatives, including disaster relief efforts and community development programs.

643.

The company has embraced digitalization and technology advancements to enhance its operations and customer experience.

644.

Dow's innovations have led to breakthroughs in medical devices, pharmaceuticals, and biotechnology.

645.

The company's commitment to ethical business practices has earned it recognition as a responsible corporate citizen.

646.

Dow has a legacy of partnering with research institutions, universities, and government agencies to drive scientific advancements.

647.

The company's commitment to circular economy principles has led to advancements in recycling and waste reduction.

648.

Dow's sustainability goals include reducing its plastic waste and enabling a more circular economy for plastics.

649.

The company's products and technologies have contributed to improving quality of life and addressing global challenges.

650.

Dow's history is a testament to its enduring commitment to innovation, sustainability, and making a positive impact on the world.

651.

Albertsons Companies is a major American grocery retail company that operates a variety of supermarket chains across the United States.

652.

The company was founded in 1939 by Joe Albertson in Boise, Idaho, with the first store opening as "Idaho's largest and finest food store."

653.

Joe Albertson's commitment to quality and customer service helped the company grow rapidly, even during the Great Depression.

654.

The original Albertsons store featured innovative concepts like a scratch bakery and an ice cream shop.

655.

The company's iconic "Lucky" brand symbol, a smiling face with a horseshoe, was designed to symbolize good luck.

656.

Albertsons was among the first supermarkets to introduce the concept of a self-service shopping experience.

657.

The company introduced the concept of "self-checkout" lanes, allowing customers to scan and pay for their items themselves.

658.

Albertsons expanded beyond its Idaho roots and opened stores in other states, eventually becoming a regional and national presence.

659.

In 1966, Albertsons introduced the "Super Saver" concept, offering lower prices on everyday items.

660.

Albertsons' growth included acquisitions of other grocery chains, expanding its market reach and customer base.

661.

In 1984, Albertsons introduced the "Preferred Savings Card," one of the earliest loyalty card programs in the grocery industry.

662.

The company continued to innovate with concepts like in-store pharmacies, floral departments, and specialty food sections.

663.

Albertsons has a history of philanthropy, including supporting local communities and charitable organizations.

664.

In 2006, Albertsons underwent a series of acquisitions and mergers, leading to its integration into the SUPERVALU Inc. umbrella.

665.

In 2013, Albertsons acquired the Albertsons stores from SUPERVALU, bringing the brand back under its control.

666.

The company has a diverse portfolio of supermarket brands, including Albertsons, Safeway, Vons, Jewel-Osco, and more.

667.

Albertsons Companies' stores cater to a wide range of customer preferences, from organic and health-focused to traditional.

668.

Albertsons has embraced digital transformation, offering online grocery shopping, delivery services, and mobile apps for convenience.

669.

The company has been recognized for its commitment to sustainability, including initiatives to reduce food waste and plastic usage.

670.

Albertsons launched the "Nourishing Neighbors" program to address hunger in local communities through partnerships with local food banks.

671.

The company has expanded its offerings to include prepared foods, deli items, and convenience options to meet changing consumer needs.

672.

Albertsons Companies has a history of adapting to consumer preferences and introducing new product categories.

673.

In 2020, Albertsons Companies went public again with an initial public offering (IPO) on the New York Stock Exchange.

674.

Albertsons continues to invest in technology, data analytics, and e-commerce capabilities to enhance the customer experience.

675.

The company's pharmacies play a vital role in providing health and wellness services to customers.

676.

Albertsons has a commitment to diversity and inclusion, promoting a culture of equality and respect for all employees.

677.

The company's private label brands offer a range of quality products across various price points.

678.

Albertsons Companies' store layouts and designs have evolved over the years to create more shopper-friendly environments.

679.

The company actively engages with customers through loyalty programs and personalized offers.

680.

Albertsons has a strong focus on employee training and development to ensure excellent customer service.

681.

The company's growth and success have been attributed to its adaptability to changing market trends and consumer preferences.

682.

Albertsons has launched initiatives to reduce its environmental footprint, including energy-efficient stores and sustainable sourcing practices.

683.

The company's commitment to quality products and customer satisfaction has earned it a loyal customer base.

684.

Albertsons supports local communities through initiatives like community fundraisers, food drives, and disaster relief efforts.

685.

The company's history reflects its ability to navigate through industry changes and economic challenges.

686.

Albertsons' diverse store formats allow it to serve urban, suburban, and rural communities across the United States.

687.

The company has a legacy of adapting to new technologies, from the introduction of barcode scanning to modern digital platforms.

688.

Albertsons has a reputation for competitive pricing, offering weekly specials and promotions to attract and retain customers.

689.

The company's loyalty programs provide personalized offers and discounts to enhance the shopping experience.

690.

Albertsons has embraced modern food trends by offering a variety of organic, gluten-free, and plant-based products.

691.

The company's store banners have become integral parts of local communities, often reflecting regional tastes and preferences.

692.

Albertsons has a strong commitment to food safety, quality assurance, and responsible sourcing.

693.

The company's "Own Brands" program offers a wide range of private-label products that meet high quality standards.

694.

Albertsons' charitable efforts extend to disaster relief, including providing support during natural disasters and emergencies.

695.

The company's stores often serve as community gathering places, offering amenities beyond grocery shopping.

696.

Albertsons' innovative approaches have set standards in the industry and influenced how supermarkets operate.

697.

The company's digital transformation has allowed customers to order groceries online, enabling convenience and accessibility.

698.

Albertsons continues to invest in modernizing its stores, enhancing customer experiences through upgraded layouts and technology.

699.

The company's ongoing commitment to customer satisfaction is reflected in its diverse offerings and dedication to service.

700.

Albertsons Companies' rich history highlights its role as a cornerstone of the American supermarket industry, adapting to changing times and customer needs.

701.

The Jonathan Sturges House, known as The Cottage, is a historic residence located in Fairfield, Connecticut.

702.

The house was built in 1840 and is considered an excellent example of the Gothic Revival architectural style.

703.

It was designed by renowned architect Alexander Jackson Davis, who was known for his contributions to the Gothic Revival movement.

704.

Jonathan Sturges, a successful merchant, commissioned the construction of the house as a summer residence for his family.

705.

The Cottage is characterized by its steeply pitched gable roof, decorative woodwork, and pointed arch windows.

706.

The house features intricate wood carvings, including decorative bargeboards, ornate brackets, and quatrefoil designs.

707.

The exterior of the house showcases a mix of materials, including wood siding, decorative shingles, and stone accents.

708.

The interior of The Cottage is equally impressive, with a layout that reflects the Victorian-era fascination with irregular shapes and designs.

709.

The house is surrounded by beautifully landscaped grounds, reflecting the 19th-century appreciation for picturesque landscapes.

710.

The Cottage is often hailed as one of the finest examples of Gothic Revival architecture in Connecticut.

711.

It was added to the National Register of Historic Places in 1973, recognizing its architectural and historical significance.

712.

The house's distinctive design and historical importance have led to its inclusion in numerous architectural and historical publications.

713.

The Jonathan Sturges House serves as a reminder of the wealth and taste of 19th-century Connecticut residents.

714.

The Cottage has been carefully preserved and restored over the years to maintain its original charm and character.

715.

The property showcases a blend of architectural influences, including Gothic, Tudor, and Victorian elements.

716.

The house is surrounded by a lush garden that complements its architectural style and enhances its visual appeal.

717.

The Cottage's Gothic Revival details, such as lancet windows and pointed arches, evoke a sense of romanticism.

718.

The property stands as a testament to the era's architectural experimentation and creativity.

719.

The house's architectural significance lies in its unique blend of historical references and artistic innovation.

720.

The Jonathan Sturges House stands as a connection to Fairfield's historical development and affluent past.

721.

The property's inclusion on the National Register of Historic Places ensures its protection and recognition.

722.

The Cottage's picturesque appearance makes it a popular subject for artists, photographers, and enthusiasts of architectural history.

723.

The house's preservation efforts demonstrate a commitment to honoring and showcasing Fairfield's cultural heritage.

724.

The property's elegant and timeless design has contributed to its status as a local and national treasure.

725.

The Cottage represents an important chapter in Fairfield's architectural legacy, reflecting the town's growth and transformation.

726.

The house's intricate woodwork and detailing highlight the craftsmanship and skills of artisans from the 19th century.

727.

The Jonathan Sturges House serves as an educational resource, offering insights into the architectural trends of the period.

728.

The property's preservation efforts serve as an inspiration for maintaining and protecting historical landmarks.

729.

The Cottage's architectural significance extends beyond its local context, resonating with architectural enthusiasts worldwide.

730.

The house's historical value is complemented by its picturesque setting, creating an inviting and tranquil environment.

731.

The Jonathan Sturges House has been featured in architectural tours and events, attracting visitors interested in history and design.

732.

The property's historical documentation and research contribute to a better understanding of 19th-century life and culture.

733.

The Cottage's graceful proportions and design principles are a testament to the enduring appeal of the Gothic Revival style.

734.

The house's preservation involves a careful balance between maintaining authenticity and ensuring structural stability.

735.

The Jonathan Sturges House has inspired discussions on architectural preservation and the importance of cultural heritage.

736.

The property has been a source of pride for the local community, fostering a sense of historical identity and belonging.

737.

The Cottage's architectural details and features showcase the skillful blending of aesthetic beauty and functional design.

738.

The house's interiors are adorned with period-appropriate furnishings, allowing visitors to step back in time.

739.

The property's unique architecture invites exploration and sparks conversations about design evolution and artistic expression.

740.

The Jonathan Sturges House is often included in Fairfield's cultural and historical programs, offering enriching experiences for visitors.

741.

The house's architectural significance transcends its function as a residence, serving as a work of art in its own right.

742.

The Cottage's longevity speaks to the quality of its construction and the care taken to ensure its preservation.

743.

The property's recognition on the National Register underscores its importance within the broader context of American architectural history.

744.

The Jonathan Sturges House embodies the romantic ideals of the 19th century, reflecting the era's fascination with the past.

745.

The house's presence serves as a link between past and present, connecting contemporary society with the values of the past.

746.

The Cottage's inviting facade and charming details contribute to its reputation as a beloved local landmark.

747.

The property's architectural significance is a testament to the collaborative efforts of architects, historians, and preservationists.

748.

The Jonathan Sturges House provides a glimpse into the lives of the individuals who inhabited it during the Victorian era.

749.

The house's enduring appeal has made it a popular subject for architectural studies and academic research.

<h1 style="text-align:center">750.</h1>

The Cottage's preservation underscores the importance of safeguarding historical structures and sharing their stories with future generations.

<h1 style="text-align:center">751.</h1>

The Ida Tarbell House is a historic residence located in Easton, Connecticut.

<h1 style="text-align:center">752.</h1>

It was the home of Ida Tarbell, a pioneering journalist, biographer, and muckraker.

<h1 style="text-align:center">753.</h1>

Ida Tarbell is best known for her investigative journalism that exposed the unethical practices of the Standard Oil Company.

<h1 style="text-align:center">754.</h1>

The house was built in the 18th century and is a fine example of Colonial architecture.

<h1 style="text-align:center">755.</h1>

Ida Tarbell purchased the house in 1915 and lived there until her death in 1944.

<h1 style="text-align:center">756.</h1>

The Ida Tarbell House was designated a National Historic Landmark in 1993.

<h1 style="text-align:center">757.</h1>

The house served as Ida Tarbell's refuge where she wrote many of her influential works.

<h1 style="text-align:center">758.</h1>

Ida Tarbell's biography of Abraham Lincoln is considered one of the most comprehensive and well-researched of its kind.

759.

The house reflects Ida Tarbell's commitment to preserving history and promoting education.

760.

The property includes a charming garden that was tended to by Ida Tarbell herself.

761.

Ida Tarbell's investigative journalism played a significant role in the Progressive Era's efforts to expose corruption and promote reform.

762.

She is credited with being one of the leading figures in the development of investigative journalism.

763.

Ida Tarbell's work on Standard Oil was published as a series of articles in McClure's Magazine and later compiled into a book.

764.

The investigative series on Standard Oil led to public outrage and contributed to the breakup of the company by antitrust laws.

765.

The Ida Tarbell House serves as a tangible link to her legacy as a journalist and a key figure in American history.

766.

The property's preservation highlights Ida Tarbell's contributions to journalism, women's history, and social reform.

767.

The house's interior includes original furnishings and personal belongings, providing insight into Ida Tarbell's life.

768.

Ida Tarbell's meticulous research and dedication to accuracy set a high standard for investigative reporting.

769.

The Ida Tarbell House is often visited by journalists, historians, and students interested in her impact on journalism.

770.

The property's status as a National Historic Landmark underscores its significance within the broader historical context.

771.

Ida Tarbell's work inspired future generations of journalists to expose injustice and seek the truth.

772.

The Ida Tarbell House showcases her commitment to intellectual pursuits and lifelong learning.

773.

The house's location in Easton, Connecticut, reflects Ida Tarbell's connection to rural New England life.

774.

Ida Tarbell's writings extended beyond investigative journalism to topics like history, biographies, and women's rights.

775.

The property's architecture and setting provide a serene backdrop for understanding Ida Tarbell's literary contributions.

776.

The Ida Tarbell House has been the site of various educational programs and events focusing on journalism and history.

777.

Ida Tarbell's influence reached beyond her lifetime, shaping the field of journalism ethics and standards.

778.

The house's preservation efforts honor Ida Tarbell's legacy as a trailblazer for women in journalism.

779.

The Ida Tarbell House serves as a reminder of the power of journalism in shaping public opinion and policy.

780.

Ida Tarbell's dedication to accuracy and thorough research earned her the reputation of a meticulous journalist.

781.

The property's gardens offer visitors a tranquil space for reflection and contemplation.

782.

Ida Tarbell's contributions to the women's suffrage movement added to her legacy as a progressive thinker.

783.

The Ida Tarbell House is a place where visitors can connect with the history of journalism and social change.

784.

Ida Tarbell's work contributed to a broader awareness of the need for government regulation of monopolies.

785.

The house stands as a testament to Ida Tarbell's commitment to justice, truth, and the pursuit of knowledge.

786.

The Ida Tarbell House has been recognized by the Connecticut Women's Hall of Fame for its historical significance.

787.

Ida Tarbell's writing style blended thorough research with compelling storytelling, engaging readers on complex topics.

788.

The house's location in a small Connecticut town contrasts with Ida Tarbell's significant impact on national issues.

789.

Ida Tarbell's investigative skills and determination challenged powerful corporations and exposed their wrongdoings.

790.

The property's preservation demonstrates the enduring relevance of Ida Tarbell's contributions to journalism.

791.

Ida Tarbell's writings are still studied in journalism and history courses, showcasing their lasting impact.

792.

The Ida Tarbell House has been featured in documentaries and literature focusing on muckraking journalism.

793.

Ida Tarbell's dedication to transparency and accountability paved the way for modern investigative reporting.

794.

The property's museum exhibits educate visitors about Ida Tarbell's life, work, and impact on American society.

795.

Ida Tarbell's biography of Napoleon Bonaparte is another example of her diverse literary achievements.

796.

The Ida Tarbell House embodies the spirit of the Progressive Era's efforts to address societal issues.

797.

Ida Tarbell's commitment to shining a light on corruption continues to inspire journalists advocating for social change.

798.

The property's historical importance extends to its role in preserving Ida Tarbell's legacy for future generations.

799.

Ida Tarbell's contributions to journalism have left an indelible mark on the field's ethics and responsibilities.

800.

The Ida Tarbell House is a place where visitors can gain a deeper understanding of the influential journalist's impact on society.

801.

Horses are part of the Equidae family and are known for their speed, strength, and endurance.

802.

Horses have been domesticated for thousands of years, with evidence of their domestication dating back to around 4000 BC.

803.

The scientific name for the domestic horse is Equus ferus caballus.

804.

Horses are herbivores, primarily feeding on grass and other vegetation.

805.

The average lifespan of a horse is around 25 to 30 years, although some horses have been known to live longer.

806.

Horses are measured in hands, with one hand equaling about four inches. The height is measured from the ground to the highest point of the withers.

807.

Horses have a unique pattern of hair known as a "whorl" or "cowlick," which is often used to identify individuals.

808.

Horses are social animals that form strong bonds with other horses and even other animals, like dogs.

809.

A male horse is called a stallion, a castrated male is a gelding, and a female horse is a mare.

810.

Horses have excellent memory, which helps them remember people, places, and experiences.

811.

The domestication of horses revolutionized human societies by providing transportation, agriculture, and military advantages.

812.

The oldest known domesticated horse remains were found in Kazakhstan and are estimated to be around 5,500 years old.

813.

Horses have a strong sense of smell and can distinguish different scents.

814.

Horses communicate with each other through body language, vocalizations, and facial expressions.

815.

Horses have a unique digestive system called hindgut fermentation, which allows them to efficiently digest fibrous plant materials.

816.

Horses have a natural flight response, which means they are often quick to react to perceived threats.

817.

The fastest recorded speed of a horse is around 55 miles per hour (88.5 kilometers per hour).

818.

Horses have a unique skeletal structure with a single toe on each foot surrounded by a hoof.

819.

Horses have a remarkable ability to learn and adapt to new tasks, which has made them invaluable in various human activities.

820.

The process of training and working with horses is known as horsemanship or horse training.

821.

Horses have a wide range of coat colors and patterns, including bay, chestnut, black, white, and various combinations.

822.

The term "horsepower" was originally coined by James Watt, the inventor of the steam engine, to market the power of his machines by comparing them to the work of horses.

823.

Horses have a complex social hierarchy within their herds, often led by a dominant mare.

824.

Horses have a blind spot directly in front of and behind them, which is why they may startle if approached suddenly from those angles.

825.

The horse's sense of hearing is highly developed, and they can rotate their ears 180 degrees to pick up sounds from various directions.

826.

Horses have a natural instinct to roll in the dust or mud, which helps keep their skin clean and repel insects.

827.

Horses have a specific sleep pattern known as "polyphasic sleep," which means they sleep in short bursts throughout the day and night.

828.

The oldest known horse fossils date back around 55 million years.

829.

Horses were initially used for food by early humans before they were domesticated for other purposes.

830.

The process of giving birth in horses is relatively quick, with foals usually standing and walking within a few hours of being born.

831.

Horses have a keen sense of touch, with many sensory receptors in their skin and lips.

832.

Horses have a strong bond with their human handlers, often recognizing their voice and scent.

833.

The practice of horse racing dates back to ancient civilizations, and it remains a popular sport around the world.

834.

Horses have been used in therapy, known as equine-assisted therapy, to help individuals with physical, emotional, and cognitive challenges.

835.

Horses' teeth continue to grow throughout their lives, which is why dental care is important for their well-being.

836.

Horses are often used in search and rescue operations due to their agility and ability to navigate various terrains.

837.

Horses' hooves are made of keratin, the same material as human fingernails.

838.

The famous Lipizzaner horses are known for their elegant performances in classical dressage routines.

839.

Horses were crucial in agriculture for plowing fields, pulling carts, and transporting goods before the advent of modern machinery.

840.

The breed known as the Arabian horse is one of the oldest and has played a significant role in the development of other breeds.

841.

Horses have a large and well-developed cecum, which helps break down fibrous plant material through fermentation.

842.

Horses have a unique galloping gait where all four feet are off the ground during certain phases of the stride.

843.

The practice of horse whispering involves using nonverbal cues and body language to communicate with horses.

844.

Horses have a special adaptation called the "stay apparatus," which allows them to lock their knees and rest while standing.

845.

The horseshoe was invented to protect horses' hooves and is made from materials like steel or aluminum.

846.

Horses played a significant role in World War I and World War II, serving as cavalry mounts and transporting supplies.

847.

The American Quarter Horse is known for its speed over short distances and its versatility in various equestrian disciplines.

848.

Horses have been depicted in art and literature throughout history, symbolizing freedom, strength, and beauty.

849.

The process of a horse giving birth is known as foaling, and it is essential for the health and survival of both the mare and foal.

850.

Horses have made a lasting impact on human culture, from ancient myths and legends to modern sports and entertainment.

851.

Horseshoe crabs are not true crabs; they belong to the class Merostomata, which is a distinct ancient arthropod lineage.

852.

They have been around for about 450 million years, making them one of the oldest living species on Earth.

853.

Horseshoe crabs have a hard exoskeleton that protects their body, and they molt as they grow.

854.

Despite their name, horseshoe crabs are more closely related to arachnids (spiders and scorpions) than to true crabs.

855.

Horseshoe crabs have a distinctive horseshoe-shaped carapace, which covers most of their body.

856.

The carapace is divided into three sections: the prosoma (head region), the opisthosoma (abdomen), and the telson (spike-like tail).

857.

Horseshoe crabs are found along the Atlantic coasts of North America, from Maine to the Gulf of Mexico, and along the Gulf of Mexico's coast.

858.

They inhabit shallow coastal waters and are often found in sandy or muddy substrate areas.

859.

Horseshoe crabs play a vital ecological role as scavengers and predators of small marine animals.

860.

The blue blood of horseshoe crabs contains a substance called Limulus amebocyte lysate (LAL), which is used to test for bacterial contamination in medical equipment and vaccines.

861.

Horseshoe crabs are not typically used for food consumption, but their eggs are an essential food source for migrating shorebirds.

862.

During spawning season, horseshoe crabs gather in large numbers on beaches to lay their eggs.

863.

Horseshoe crab eggs are green due to the presence of a unique molecule called biliverdin, which also gives them antibacterial properties.

864.

The eggs are laid in nests in the sand and provide a crucial energy source for shorebirds during their migration.

865.

The population of horseshoe crabs has been declining due to habitat loss, pollution, and overharvesting.

866.

Horseshoe crabs have ten eyes that help them detect light and movement, but their vision is relatively poor.

867.

They use their long tail (telson) to flip themselves over if they end up upside down.

868.

Male horseshoe crabs are generally smaller than females, and they have specialized front legs to grasp onto females during mating.

869.

Mating occurs during high tide, with the male attaching to the female's back and fertilizing the eggs as she lays them.

870.

Horseshoe crabs are not aggressive and are harmless to humans. Their tail is not a stinger; it's used for stability and steering.

871.

Despite their ancient appearance, horseshoe crabs are not considered "living fossils" but rather a part of an ancient lineage that has evolved over time.

872.

The extinct eurypterids, commonly known as sea scorpions, are distant relatives of horseshoe crabs and were much larger.

873.

Horseshoe crabs have a limited ability to regenerate lost limbs, mainly during their molting process.

874.

The Atlantic horseshoe crab (Limulus polyphemus) is the most well-known species, but there are three other species found in different parts of the world.

875.

Horseshoe crabs play a critical role in the food web by consuming detritus and small organisms, and they provide a food source for various predators.

876.

Their eggs provide essential nutrients to coastal ecosystems, supporting both marine and terrestrial species.

877.

The horseshoe crab's blood is used in the LAL test, which detects bacterial endotoxins and ensures the safety of medical equipment and vaccines.

878.

Horseshoe crab populations have been protected and managed through regulations to ensure their conservation and sustainable use.

879.

Fossils of horseshoe crabs reveal that their appearance hasn't changed significantly over millions of years.

880.

The horseshoe crab's respiratory system involves book gills, specialized appendages that extract oxygen from the water.

881.

The Atlantic horseshoe crab's blood is blue when oxygenated due to the presence of copper-based hemocyanin.

882.

Horseshoe crab eggs are considered a delicacy in some Asian cuisines and are used in dishes like sushi.

883.

Despite their name, horseshoe crabs are not used for horseshoe making and are not related to horses.

884.

The horseshoe crab's eggs are an essential resource for the Delaware Bay ecosystem, where hundreds of thousands of migrating shorebirds depend on them.

885.

In some cultures, horseshoe crabs are considered good luck symbols and are even kept as pets in aquariums.

886.

Horseshoe crabs have been used as bait in the fishing industry due to their strong smell and oily texture.

887.

The horseshoe crab's carapace provides protection, but it can also have algae and other organisms growing on it.

888.

They are sensitive to changes in their environment, making them valuable indicators of environmental health.

889.

Horseshoe crabs are often referred to as "living fossils" because of their ancient lineage and relatively unchanged appearance.

890.

The horseshoe crab's compound eyes are well-adapted for detecting movement and changes in light.

891.

The name "horseshoe crab" comes from the shape of their carapace, which resembles a horseshoe.

892.

Horseshoe crabs have a prehistoric appearance, often sparking interest and fascination among people.

893.

Horseshoe crabs molt their exoskeleton several times during their lives, and after molting, their color is often dull until the new exoskeleton hardens.

894.

The horseshoe crab's telson is not a stinger, but it's used to help the crab flip itself over if it gets stranded on its back.

895.

Horseshoe crabs have been studied for their potential use in developing new antibiotics and antiviral medications.

896.

Their reproductive behaviors and migrations are essential for maintaining coastal ecosystems' balance and health.

897.

The horseshoe crab's eggs are not only essential for shorebirds but also contribute to the overall biodiversity of coastal habitats.

898.

In some cultures, horseshoe crabs are considered sacred animals and are even used in traditional ceremonies.

899.

Horseshoe crabs have played a significant role in scientific research, providing insights into evolution, neurobiology, and immunology.

900.

Efforts are ongoing to protect and conserve horseshoe crab populations to ensure their ecological and medical significance for future generations.

901.

UnitedHealth Group (UHG) is an American multinational managed healthcare company headquartered in Minnetonka, Minnesota.

902.

The company was founded on October 1, 1977, by Richard T. Burke as Charter Med Incorporated, focusing on providing health coverage for individuals.

903.

In 1979, the company changed its name to United Healthcare Corporation.

904.

United Healthcare initially operated with a network of doctors and hospitals, offering medical coverage to consumers.

905.

UHG's growth was fueled by acquisitions, allowing it to expand its services and geographic reach.

906.

In 1984, United Healthcare became publicly traded on the New York Stock Exchange.

907.

The company's acquisition of MetraHealth in 1995 marked a significant expansion into the dental and vision benefits market.

908.

United Healthcare's acquisition of Oxford Health Plans in 2004 further strengthened its presence in the health insurance industry.

909.

In 2008, the company adopted the name UnitedHealth Group to reflect its diverse range of health-related services.

910.

UnitedHealth Group operates through two main divisions: UnitedHealthcare for health benefits and Optum for health services.

911.

Optum was created in 2011 to consolidate the company's growing portfolio of health services, technology, and consulting businesses.

912.

UHG's Optum division provides services like healthcare analytics, pharmacy benefit management, and healthcare delivery solutions.

913.

Optum also includes OptumRx, one of the largest pharmacy benefit management companies in the United States.

914.

The company has consistently ranked among the top health insurance companies by revenue and market capitalization.

915.

UHG expanded its international presence by acquiring Amil Participações S.A., a Brazilian healthcare company, in 2012.

916.

UnitedHealth Group's services extend to health management solutions, wellness programs, and patient engagement initiatives.

917.

The company emphasizes data analytics and technology to improve healthcare outcomes and reduce costs.

918.

UnitedHealth Group is a Fortune 500 company and has consistently been recognized for its innovation and leadership in the healthcare industry.

919.

In 2018, UHG's Optum division acquired DaVita Medical Group, a leading medical group in the United States.

920.

The acquisition of DaVita Medical Group expanded UnitedHealth's provider network and enhanced its healthcare delivery capabilities.

921.

UnitedHealth Group is known for its involvement in numerous community outreach and philanthropic initiatives.

922.

The company's CEO, David S. Wichmann, has played a pivotal role in driving its strategic direction and growth.

923.

UnitedHealth Group has faced criticism and legal challenges related to its reimbursement practices, utilization management, and network policies.

924.

The company has a significant presence in the Affordable Care Act (ACA) health insurance exchanges.

925.

UHG has consistently invested in research and development to advance healthcare technology, data analytics, and patient-centered care models.

926.

UnitedHealth Group's OptumLabs is a collaborative research and innovation center that focuses on improving healthcare quality and efficiency.

927.

The company's Optum360 division offers revenue cycle management and analytics solutions for healthcare providers.

928.

UnitedHealth Group has been recognized as one of the World's Most Admired Companies by Fortune magazine.

929.

The company's acquisition of Change Healthcare in 2021 further bolstered its healthcare technology and analytics capabilities.

930.

UHG's OptumServe division provides healthcare services to government agencies, military veterans, and public health programs.

931.

UnitedHealth Group's commitment to diversity and inclusion is reflected in its workforce and corporate practices.

932.

The company's Optum Ventures division invests in startups and innovations that align with its healthcare goals.

933.

UnitedHealth Group has been involved in partnerships and initiatives to combat healthcare disparities and improve healthcare access.

934.

The company's OptumRx division manages pharmacy benefits for millions of individuals across the United States.

935.

UHG has been a vocal advocate for value-based care models and population health management..

936.

The COVID-19 pandemic highlighted the company's role in providing telehealth services and supporting public health efforts.

937.

UnitedHealth Group's focus on prevention and wellness aligns with its broader goal of improving health outcomes.

938.

The company's OptumCare division operates medical practices that provide comprehensive care coordination to patients.

939.

UHG's data analytics capabilities play a crucial role in identifying trends, managing costs, and enhancing patient care.

940.

UnitedHealth Group has a strong commitment to ethical business practices and corporate social responsibility.

941.

The company's UnitedHealth Foundation supports initiatives aimed at improving health and well-being in communities.

942.

UHG's technology solutions aim to simplify healthcare administration, enhance patient engagement, and streamline operations.

943.

UnitedHealth Group's research and innovation efforts aim to transform healthcare delivery through technology, analytics, and data-driven insights.

944.

The company's Medicare and Medicaid offerings provide healthcare coverage to millions of seniors and low-income individuals.

945.

UHG's OptumInsight division focuses on health information technology, revenue cycle management, and consulting services.

946.

UnitedHealth Group's investments in digital health solutions align with industry trends toward virtual care and telemedicine.

947.

The company's commitment to sustainability is evident in its efforts to reduce its environmental footprint and promote responsible business practices.

948.

UHG's OptumHealth division delivers personalized care management and wellness solutions to improve individual health outcomes.

949.

UnitedHealth Group's ongoing acquisitions and partnerships reflect its commitment to advancing healthcare innovation.

950.

As a leader in the healthcare industry, UnitedHealth Group continues to shape the future of healthcare through its diverse portfolio of services and commitment to improving health outcomes for individuals and communities.

951.

Morgan Stanley is a global investment bank and financial services firm headquartered in New York City, founded in 1935.

952.

The firm was formed by the merger of J.P. Morgan & Co. and the original Morgan Stanley in 1935, resulting in the name "Morgan Stanley."

953.

The merger was a response to the Glass-Steagall Act, which required a separation of commercial and investment banking activities.

954.

The firm's original founders included Henry S. Morgan, Harold Stanley, and others from J.P. Morgan & Co.

955.

The company initially focused on investment banking and securities trading, aiming to provide financial services to corporations, institutions, and individuals.

956.

Morgan Stanley played a significant role in helping finance and advise major corporations during the industrial boom of the mid-20th century.

957.

The firm became a leader in underwriting initial public offerings (IPOs) and corporate bond issuance.

958.

In the 1980s, Morgan Stanley played a pivotal role in the development of the mortgage-backed securities market.

959.

In the late 1990s, Morgan Stanley expanded its presence in the technology sector, particularly during the dot-com boom.

960.

The firm established the Morgan Stanley Technology Investment Banking Group to focus on technology-related deals.

961.

Morgan Stanley is known for its involvement in high-profile mergers and acquisitions, including advising on the AOL-Time Warner merger.

962.

The firm also played a role in the privatization of state-owned enterprises in various countries during the 1980s and 1990s.

963.

In the 1990s, Morgan Stanley acquired Dean Witter Reynolds and Discover Financial Services, expanding its retail and brokerage services.

964.

The firm's Dean Witter acquisition led to the formation of the Morgan Stanley Dean Witter name.

965.

In 2001, the firm changed its name back to Morgan Stanley.

966.

The early 2000s saw Morgan Stanley involved in complex financial transactions, including collateralized debt obligations (CDOs).

967.

During the global financial crisis of 2008, Morgan Stanley, like other financial institutions, faced challenges due to exposure to risky assets.

968.

In response to the crisis, the U.S. government provided financial support to Morgan Stanley through the Troubled Asset Relief Program (TARP).

969.

The firm later repaid the TARP funds and strengthened its financial position.

970.

In the aftermath of the financial crisis, Morgan Stanley underwent significant restructuring to reduce risk and enhance its capital position.

971.

Morgan Stanley has a strong presence in investment banking, wealth management, asset management, and trading.

972.

The firm's wealth management division offers financial advisory services and investment solutions to high-net-worth individuals and families.

973.

Morgan Stanley's institutional securities division is involved in trading, investment banking, and advisory services for corporations and institutions.

974.

The company's asset management division manages various investment funds and strategies for institutional and individual clients.

975.

In recent years, Morgan Stanley has been actively pursuing sustainability and responsible investing initiatives.

976.

The firm has been recognized for its diversity and inclusion efforts, focusing on promoting a diverse workforce and inclusive culture.

977.

Morgan Stanley has a history of supporting philanthropic and social impact initiatives through its foundation and employee engagement programs.

978.

The firm played a role in advising on major mergers and acquisitions in the healthcare and pharmaceutical industries.

979.

In 2020, Morgan Stanley announced the acquisition of E*TRADE Financial, expanding its presence in the retail brokerage space.

980.

The company has a global presence with offices and operations in numerous countries around the world.

981.

Morgan Stanley has been ranked among the leading investment banks in terms of deal volume and revenue.

982.

The firm is listed on the New York Stock Exchange under the ticker symbol "MS."

983.

Morgan Stanley has been involved in various initiatives to advance fintech innovation and digital transformation in financial services.

984.

The company's research division provides analysis and insights on financial markets, industries, and economic trends.

985.

Morgan Stanley's trading desks cover a wide range of financial instruments, including equities, fixed income, currencies, and commodities.

986.

The firm's commitment to corporate governance and risk management has evolved over the years, especially after regulatory changes post-2008.

987.

Morgan Stanley has been recognized as one of the World's Most Admired Companies by Fortune magazine.

988.

The firm's involvement in philanthropy includes initiatives related to education, healthcare, and environmental sustainability.

989.

Morgan Stanley's impact investing efforts aim to generate positive social and environmental outcomes alongside financial returns.

990.

The firm's advisory services encompass areas like mergers and acquisitions, restructuring, capital raising, and strategic planning.

991.

Morgan Stanley actively participates in conferences and industry events to share insights and engage with clients and stakeholders.

992.

The firm's commitment to innovation is reflected in its efforts to embrace technology and explore new business models.

993.

Morgan Stanley's research analysts cover a wide range of sectors, providing insights to help clients make informed investment decisions.

994.

The firm's leadership team plays a critical role in shaping its strategic direction and navigating the challenges of the financial industry.

995.

Morgan Stanley has been recognized for its efforts to create a more sustainable financial system and support the transition to a low-carbon economy.

996.

The firm's institutional clients include corporations, governments, asset managers, and other financial institutions.

997.

Morgan Stanley has been a pioneer in developing financial products and solutions tailored to the needs of institutional clients.

998.

The firm's involvement in community development includes programs that promote financial literacy and economic empowerment.

999.

Morgan Stanley has received awards and recognition for its commitment to innovation, diversity, and corporate social responsibility.

1000.

The history of Morgan Stanley is marked by its evolution from a merger of two prominent financial institutions to becoming a global leader in investment banking, wealth management, and financial services.